Praise for

AN ABSENCE OF FEAR

"A delightful and stirring discovery, these love poems and elegies of Holly Peppe. Her gifts as a lyric poet include a rare balance of epigrammatic wit with deep passion and tenderness. Her crystalline stanzas juxtaposing love and death linger in the memory: there is nothing greater we can ask of our poets than such resonance."

Daniel Mark Epstein is the author of twenty books of poetry, biography, history, and the upcoming *Constellations: Collected Poems* (LSU Press, 2025)

"Holly Peppe's *An Absence of Fear* is filled with tenderness, undisguised longing for love, and a simultaneous acceptance of, and protest against, death. This book, which we understand as we read will probably be Peppe's last, wanders the past and the future. Carrying us into death watches and to moments of uncontainable eros, her poems cleave to Malebranche's beautiful notion that 'attention is the natural prayer of the soul.' The casual tone of the final section is in disarming, evocative tension with a cancer diagnosis it both chronicles and defies. There is no bravura, just the courage of someone seeking to describe both the outer and inner worlds with regard and humor."

Catherine Barnett is the author of four collections of poetry, including *Human Hours* and *Solutions for the Problem of Bodies in Space*

"To experience Holly Peppe's poetic vision is a profound gift. Her singular sensitivity, compassion, and largesse of spirit make for a collection that is as elegant and unassuming as the bird that occupies her first childhood poem: the swan. There are phrases here—'pale mornings breaking lonely'—that I will return to forever, with gratitude for Peppe's devotion to poetry, to beauty, to life."

Lindsay Whalen is a Leon Levy Center for Biography fellow and author of the forthcoming biography of Mary Oliver

"Writer and editor Holly Peppe has generously given us nearly a hundred heartfelt poems about love and death told with searing honesty and fierce courage as well as penetrating intelligence. Her joy in the beauty of the light or the sky or her lake is poignant as she reminds us that our perceptions, and especially hers, are impermanent and passing."

Laurie Lisle is a biographer and a memoirist whose latest book is *Word for Word: A Writer's Life*

"Holly Peppe is an artist with words. She knows how to work the beauty and power of language. This book is not just a long overdue gift to herself but a gift to everyone who loves poetry written with heart and mind and craft. It offers poems like moonlight showing the way."

Jonathan Cohen is a poet, translator, scholar, author of *Muna Lee: A Pan-American Life,* and translator of Pedro Mir's *Poems of Good Love … and Sometimes Fantasy*

"In the elegant lines of these poems, Holly Peppe finds unillusioned insights in visual images: 'flowering trees and jasmine and sweet women and pearls' suggest the 'myths you believed until now.' The birds seen 'From My First Avenue Window' remind the poet that she is 'suspended between / good health / and death.' A lifetime of observation, thought, and craft has inspired this volume of honest, beautiful poems."

Lucy McDiarmid is a scholar and writer. Her most recent monograph is *At Home in the Revolution: What Women Said and Did in 1916;* her book on contemporary Irish poetry is forthcoming in 2025

"This extraordinary collection of poems manages to reveal both the poet's absence of fear and an abundance of life. Peppe's clarity, courage, humor, wisdom, and love for nature resound through her lines, opening the way to her active mind and loving heart."

Mimi White is the author of four collections of poems including *The Last Island*, winner of the Jane Kenyan Award for Outstanding Poetry, and *The Arc Remains*

"Where do we find the confidence to live, to find meaning, to communicate, in the face of the excruciating truth of absence, of nothingness? All of us, most of the time, must wall off anxiety by turning to our numbing routines, or to religion or old myths to help us come to terms with what we cannot know. The more courageous of us, by delving into the grace of their experiences through poetic language, are able to glide upon the surface of oblivion and sing the song of being and non-being for all of us, as Holly Peppe does, in this swan song of a life lived in poetry."

Thomas E. Hill, Vassar College Art Librarian, Professor of English, and host of the Library Café, is the author of a study of Chaucer's *Troilus and Criseyde* and a commemorative edition of Edna St. Vincent Millay's poems, *Take Up the Song*

"If you take your eyes off a page just for a moment, it will take you several moments to refocus, to get your bearings back in line with the language on the page, language that functions like sleight of hand. Gorgeous on its surface, yet equally beautiful to its depths. These poems are exquisite and magically lucid—unclouded, sun-glinted, and luminous. Holly Peppe's wisdom seems unforced and purely graceful, yet she never once backs down from disclosures or ruminations—the difficulties of love, illness, aging...the difficulties of living. *An Absence of Fear* is a big-hearted, transcendent volume brimming with treasures. I am in awe of this book and would catalogue it as a must-read."

John L. Stanizzi is the author of fourteen books of poems and a forthcoming memoir

**WAXWING
ISLAND
PRESS**

www.amplifypublishinggroup.com

An Absence of Fear

The views and opinions expressed in this book are solely those of the
author. These views and opinions do not necessarily represent those
of the publisher or staff.

Cover painting, *Marchmont House Tree*, by Melinda Plant.
Reproduced for publication with permission from the artist.
Acrylic, oil, copper leaf, molding paste on canvas.

For more information, please contact:
Waxwing Island Press, an imprint of Amplify Publishing Group
620 Herndon Parkway, Suite 220
Herndon, VA 20170
info@amplifypublishing.com

Library of Congress Control Number: 2024917079

CPSIA Code: PRV0924A

ISBN-13: 979-8-89138-397-5

Printed in the United States

For Scot Hadley Evans

ALSO BY HOLLY PEPPE

An
ABSENCE
of
FEAR

poems

HOLLY PEPPE

WAXWING
ISLAND
PRESS

CONTENTS

II. LOST VOICES

III. IN DIFFERENT LIGHTS

IV. GATHERING STRENGTH

V. BLOOD TIES

VI. TERMINAL BENEFITS

Foreword

When we are on that cusp, continuing to live and simultaneously die, we are distilled to out-of-body essentials. Mortality, meanwhile, takes on an entity like a Roman god or goddess. It raises its goddess arm, and we become stripped down to memory and the moon.

Here in this lifetime of poems, Holly Peppe shows us this simple truth, that we hold within us the significant moments of our observations, those we love and have loved, and those who came before us.

What are we? Holly's poems reveal we are that look out the window at patches of snow. We are the red-tailed hawk that sucks sustenance out of the carefully laid eggs of the dove. The cat who carries a wren in its mouth. The door left open so the father will return. The last moment of consciousness of the friend struck dead by a car on Park Avenue. The Italian grandfather sitting in a chair under a red maple tree. The mother's voice in the night, chasing nightmares from the room. The companion in roller skating. The lover who can never leave us, though he is no more.

Our lives are not our lives only, but the lives of everything we have seen and remember, and all the lives that touch us—be that on the sidewalks of Rome or in the strange competition of worst-case scenarios among cancer diagnoses in oncology waiting rooms. We are in the poems that we read and quote to ourselves in times of need, in hope, in loss of hope, and in grand synergy. Poems that for us may be like the mother's voice in the night or the slice of silver that appears when we look up at the stars and the moon.

I last saw Holly when we gathered armfuls of cut flowers together and wrapped them in wet newspaper at a sink, while standing side by side and conferring. We were preparing the flowers so I could bring them to a friend of mine who was buried in a churchyard just down the hill. I turned to Holly and saw her beautiful face, lit by the soft light of the window. "How lovely you think / I'll remember this forever."

Barbara Bair

Barbara Bair is the curator of the papers of Walt Whitman, Edna St. Vincent Millay, Mary Oliver, Ai Ogawa, Muriel Rukeyser, and other poets at the Library of Congress

Poet

As a child
she spoke in images—

maple trees
reaching their arms
to the sky

waves
shimmering
like sapphires

Though unwell now,
she's still at it:

I'm like a butterfly,
she whispers,
pretty in the morning
gone by afternoon.

Introduction

My mother kept my first poem, written when I was five, in her top bureau drawer for years, tucked between linen hankies embroidered with red roses and lily of the valley:

When I grow up I want to be a swan,
and swim around in a great big pond.
And to my husband I will wave my wing,
to show him that I am a beautiful thing.

She read poetry to me before bed every night, and inspired by her love for the beauty and power of language, I've spent the rest of my life writing poems that have helped me make sense of the complexities of the human predicament. Together they are a brief record of my existence on Earth, told from the heart.

But nothing could have prepared me for learning several months ago that I have a rare incurable illness that will shorten my life. At first the news felt like a death sentence, a walk with my shadow in the dark. But because I love my life so much and have more to do before leaving the planet, I've chosen a different metaphor for the future: walking with my shadow beside a lake in a bright, clear light—my desire to live—that's still shining. Imagining that light has somehow transformed my lifelong lack of confidence in sharing my poems into a new state of mind: an absence of fear.

So here they are. I hope some of these lines will resonate with you and perhaps even shine a bright light on your life and all its wonders too.

Holly Peppe
South Salem, New York
August 2024

I.

SOJOURN

"If you ask me what my poetry is I must tell you I don't know;
but if you ask my poetry, it will tell you who I am."
—Pablo Neruda

Ascending Stairs

Summer again: flowering trees and jasmine and sweet
women and pearls
stud the landscape with myths you believed until now.
Until now, nights were all the same.

In dreams you live safely in danger.

You wake inside the body of a stranger—
the man beside you on the bus, or at an old friend's funeral.
You work nights in a factory of dreamers,
sipping hope in broken English,
drunk with an unevenness of fear.

Sunday mornings you pull the bell rope three times to
signal God.
One note forms a circle that awaits a closing,
dividing in two the road.
Another weaves light across abandoned farms
like a catbird singing the dark.
The last is release.
You begin to understand why souls faint and bleed.
You run home
to check your closet
for loaded guns.

You wake to find that your hands and legs are broken.
Your maid is Jamaican and you are her charge.
You recall playing ivory-keyed jazz for a man
that only she clearly remembers.
All day she avoids you.
Upstairs at night, she drinks wine and dark visions.

Just before dawn, her eyes cracked like bones,
she appears at your window, arranging her weapons:
a pen knife, a watch, paper cups full of leaves.

You awaken to walk down the avenue, worrying about your
clothes.
Store windows form a fence that keeps you whole.
Of late, when you look at the clock, morning sways
backward toward night.
Your lovers are a liquid of voices and hands
that refuse to leave or belong.
Sensing a difference between soil and earth,
you discover the wind wears a clue.

Summer night turned myth, warm myth turned stone,
you awaken, unable to speak.
After years and years of night you rise,
your body still moist from the gifts of your sleep.

Crescent

Above a jagged ridge of night
she rises—
a woman caped in silver—stunning
against the trees.

Like a solitary sun
glowing on dismal seas
day after timeless day—
she dilutes shadow,
strews light over blackened plains,
over mountains stripped to sheerness
over lakes, naked in their blueness
over deserts vast with thirst.

The earth a swell of night below,
she rises, fearless,
a silver silhouette
etched on darkest moon.

On Rilke's Dolls

In my last dark life
I was a shoemaker in Chicago
I mended shoes, I mended dolls
I ripped off ears, I sewed on eyes
I swallowed cloth to salvage hue
Until the night you said goodbye
the night you lied, the night you left
I lost my hearing
and my sight

Hospital Waiting Room

Easy to tell patients from visitors
We're the thin ones

I for one
am looking a little gaunt
but strive to appear hopeful
to new families
armed with cellphones and magazines
to pass the time

When they look my way
I half smile and nod
as if to say

Relax, honey
it could be worse
you could be me

Detour

"Take this detour with me"
I tell you
as if it's an order and not a question,
as if I didn't really mean
"Listen, I can't take this road alone."

In reply you relate a dream:
you are in a forest
in search of stone
when a burst of color
flings you to the ground.

Either we talk this way,
in symbols, in lines
that wend and weave,
or else we follow signs:

threads of marrow
wind
strips of bone
rain
chips of self
splinters
burned-out barns
knots of love.

Rooms

In my own quiet way
I am moving from room to room
wide and spacious rooms
rooms without windows
mirrored rooms
rooms like shoeboxes with no bed or light
rooms that never change
rooms that comfort dark
like shadows
like restless death
like hospitals

Birdsong

In Tripi, Greece, villagers await the song of the nightingale that signifies the coming of spring.

Not that the nightingales had forgotten to sing
nor that April and May had neglected to warm us
nor even that spring had deprived us of light.
But had the moon formed a tiny sliver of silver in the sky,
we might have heard those small birds sing
and more, we might have sung.

Clocks

"Do not neglect the echo. You live by echoes."
—Edmond Jabès, *The Book of Questions*

Removed from one another
like auctioned clocks
bought and sold at whim,
carried from city to village,
village to town,
placed on table or mantle
to announce the morning, welcome the night—
muted by rooms full of voices and things,
ours is a chiming of Necessity,
of Distance, the keeper of miles.

Loneliness of Road

Trees with rattling roots
hearth in a suitcase
the uncluttered loneliness of road

Crossing the Walt Whitman Bridge into Philly:
abandoned rail cars, auto junkyards, loaded barges,
Whitman like a cloud floating through greasy smog,
his finger pointing my way.
Driving over Chesapeake Bay,
I check into an off-season beach hotel.
Walking the desolate beach,
I meet Demetrius, an out-of-work chef
who says the acropolis was built
with hammers no bigger than seashells,
the Parthenon was never finished
because the architect died.

Later, in a Newport News shipyard,
sharing almonds and raisins
with a Russian waitress
who calls me Baby,
I hold fast to Buddhist wisdom:
"We learn when we wander alone."

Secondary Yearnings

For light years you pretend that moments are suns
rising to warm you. You laugh when you run out of fear.
There are no answers to dreams.

Rivers are scarce for want to rain; a dawn sky rises
wide with causes. Though mountain streams
course to valley pools,
no rivers form.

All this, all this because of you.

New England January

Patches of snow
on black earth
viewed from your window
calls back all
you cannot understand,
though the space between endings
traces its thin hope backward
to hold your attention,
traces straight and silent
a skeleton tree
alone in a winter field.

Vienna, 1933

At seventy-seven, Freud
spoke flawless English,
placed a small, bronze statue
of Pallas Athena
on his palm,
calling her "imperfect
because she had
lost her spear."

To reclaim her place
in the Professor's scheme,
she must wince or break:
she did not.

Nor had mighty Zeus winced
or broken apart
when she sprang
from his head-womb
armed for war.

But for wings
she was one with angels,
but for a spear,
one with Freud.

Not That Distance Makes the Heart

Not that distance makes the heart
do anything special, but that thought,
the mind's touch and sight, turns your voice
into such fresh memory, it's as if
you still stood at the door,
ready to leave.
For whatever reason the mind discards
most of what it receives,
but records and preserves brief moments
like these forever,
it has fixed a place for you here—
still moving away from me,
saying goodbye.

Ask Me to Stop Loving You

Ask me
to stop loving you.

Then ask spring violets
to hold fast
each purple bud.
Ask pear trees not to blossom.

I try to let go.

A bluejay poses
mid-air
above the feeder.
A chipmunk clings
motionless
to the rock below.

The cat,
a wren in his mouth,
stalks the new-mown lawn.

Loving and Dying

In many ways
loving
is like dying.
In love
you are always alone,
trying not to suffer,
striving for dignity,
for simple answers.
There are no chairs,
no walls
to hold you
upright.
In love
it is all windows
and stairways.

As in death,
silence matters most:
the saving of words,
the strategy
of burying
unspoken anger.

Loving is only easy
for sturdy hearts
that know how

and when
to soften;
it's never easy
for hearts that burst
with excruciating truth
as in death.
Again and again
in loving and dying,
we ask ourselves if <u>this</u>
is really <u>it</u>.

Falling in love is private,
even lonely.
After that
you're always guarded
but cannot hide.
Those who had shunned you
pull close to watch your despairs:
choosing the unchosen,
loving the wrong person
the wrong way.
You learn quickly:
the isolation of hard loving
is like dying.
In the end
no one
will forgive you.

II.

LOST VOICES

"All death has one glance."
—Cesare Pavese

Jotting a Note to the World

You ask forgiveness.
Forgetting that I have no tongue,
I try to answer.

You ask my mother's name;
I falter, cannot recall it.
You say your second sight is keen;
mine is growing. Still
I cannot locate my mouth.

You will say I have no voice,
no sensibility.
My fingers probe the space above my chin;
it is difficult to love you.

For Maxine

On the last night of the year
when winter closed us in from sight,
we sat there talking,
praying for you.
Let there be light, we prayed,
let there be her special light.

You were his lifeline, Pawel told me,
sitting in the cluttered parlor,
questioning hope.
Gray smoke lingered there where we waited
that cold white icy night.

These days, Maxine, I live in Rome
where nothing is forgotten
at early dusk when church bells clamor.
Tonight the spring's full moon
is lighting your way to us,
calling you home.

In Borghese Park

In Borghese Park in winter,
a boy is making a grave for a bird,
a bird—he is certain—has no father or mother.

Today I saw a black-haired boy
leading a cat on a leash
through the streets of Rome.
His hands were small and red from the cold
but he sang for my coins with the heart of a man.

Beyond the thin-limbed winter trees,
beyond the frozen pond,
beyond the boys
whose fingers burn with cold:
a wind that carries sadnesses
across the graves of birds.

For Pawel

Landscapes are wide, rivers endless and cool,
waters green like the spruce forests close to the sea,
flowing like hope.

Time heals loss, they are telling you now,
though your grief is too dark for such promise
or prayer.
Still they say this again to you,
over and over:

We cannot guide stars
or the fierce wind of death
or anything, in fact, but our small daily lives.

Given over to starlight and dust,
time's all she's left you,
souvenir
not of a mingling of spheres
but of clash.

Spring Song

Lost to the sky, sparrows recall
nests of strength, beginnings.
Lost to meadows, skylarks wing
from beds of sweet heather
to mountains and seas.
Birds know that life cannot last,
as you did, crossing dusk for night.

Consolation

All night beyond two sturdy shutters
stray dogs bark sharp in leaps of fright,
unpredictable frantic sounds.
But you are disembodied now, you know
that you have suffered much, you know
that truth does not equal philosophy.

The truth you know resounds again:
we are smaller than the fragile bones
of birds with wobbly legs
who neither sing nor scorn the silences
that glorify their flight.

The Monk Is Dead

for Thelonious Monk (1917–1982)

They said now that The Monk is dead,
it's always after midnight,
beyond the trees and sidewalks
there's no more seeing
light. It's all the time the thinnest moon,
nights darker than his moving hands.
Today they said The Monk is dead.
I tell you friend,
they're liars.

Night Letter to Carole

"Carole Honig Klein, a biographer and author of other nonfiction works, died on Monday from injuries after being struck by a car on the Upper East Side. She was 67 and lived in Manhattan. She had recently lost her husband of 45 years."—New York Times, July 4, 2001

Everyone says it's unbelievable
That you were here yesterday
And now
No matter where we look
No matter who we call
We cannot find you

Everyone I ask
Says they just spoke with you
Or were about to call you
When suddenly
Without warning
You disappeared

The last time I saw you
We had dinner with a friend
And talked all the way home
In a taxi
You told me you hoped
Things would be better soon
Though you had your doubts

I assured you time would heal your loss
As it always does to some degree

What you were thinking today
As you walked into traffic
While crossing Park Avenue
None of us who love you
Will ever know for sure

Nor can we bear to imagine
The terror you felt
In that crazy, confusing swirl
Of skids and noise
Before merciful darkness descended.

In the West Indies they would say
You were distracted
When your husband
Called out your name

"Please come to me, my darling"
He was calling
Which startled you for an instant
As you stood straight and still
So full of joy to hear his voice

So full of joy
In that brief, awful moment
As full as we are now
Of sorrow

Yet we are hopeful too
You are no longer alone
But resting in his arms again
Surrounded by love.

Icarus Redux

Early this morning
when a huge red-tailed hawk
drove the dappled mourning dove
from her nest in the fir tree
outside my window,
and pierced two warm, white eggs
and sucked them dry,
no one made a move
to stop him:
not the glittering blue butterfly
sipping nectar
in the cornflowers,
or the sleek gray squirrel
flying wildly from tree to tree,
or the sculpted stone rabbit
watching intently
from the garden below,
waiting patiently
until nightfall
when he could
close his eyes.

Letter to Pilot Steve Fossett

Thank you for proving
once and for all
that the world is not flat,
days are not endless,
and our lives,
no matter how noble or daring
or willful or bold,
have a takeoff and landing,
a beginning
and an end.

Circling low,
studying every mile
of rugged terrain,
pilots and search crews
flew hundreds of hours
looking for a sign you had touched down.
Their hopes rising and falling
in the unforgiving High Sierra,
how could they know
they were searching in vain?

How could they know
you'd had other plans?

Breaking new records
for altitude and courage,
you soared straight upward
miraculous in flight,
your single-engine plane
finally breaking through
to the lower reaches of a place
higher than the sky
where the air is as thin and pure
as a slender sliver of light,
so perfectly formed
and undeniably beautiful
that it made you smile
just moments before you disappeared.

Elegy in D Minor

Forgive me, Anna,
for not attending your funeral,
for pretending I was ill,
for hiding in my study,
sipping the brandy you gave me
at two o'clock, when the service began.

For not answering the phone for a week afterward,
for repeating your name softly,
then louder and louder to no one,
for this hollow feeling,
for these apologies,
forgive me, please.

That I should wish you alive today,
hammering out tunes on an off-key piano,
music as old as those bleak rented rooms;
that I should long for one more hour
trading smokes and jazz and histories:
these are thoughts too futile
to pursue.

Only forgive please the stillness,
the evening's stealthy drift toward blindness.
Forgive me
the inability
to refrain from words
at a time like this.

Grief

When my dog Ringo Jack died,
a piece of my heart
went with him.

But that's not really true.

It was my whole heart
And a tiny sliver of soul
I didn't know I had.

Eulogy for Arachne:
Notes from a Brave Spider's Funeral

"Please stand!" the elder spider cried
to rows of mourners gathered close
beneath a well-trod farmhouse floor.
On twenty thousand legs they rose.

From every corner of the house,
from every crevice 'neath the eves,
from gardens, barn, from woodpile too,
they'd come to mourn Arachne.

Proud pastor of Allspiderboro,
the wise old spider faced the crowd.
"A sad occasion here," he cried,
"Arachne sacrificed her life
for want of friendship from a race
of heavy voices, hearts, and shoes.

"Though our Praying Mantis cousin's seen
a blessing by these tree-legged beasts,
though Daddy-Longlegs brings them luck
and chocolate ants are treasured feasts,
no matter how we toil and spin
or decorate with lacy threads
to beautify an empty house,
we're seen a threat to floor-high beds.

"Arachne knew, yet took the chance,
her tiny, practiced song too soft
to make amends for scornful eyes
perpetuating spite for spiders'
hairy, scary legs and arms.

"Arachne knew, yet faced her foe
like Beowulf, like Cuchulain—
undaunted by the monster shape
that loomed before her late that night,
the night her spider-Godforsaken frame
was crushed asunder.

"No truer web has e'er been spun
than the one she hoped would foster peace:
a long-awaited truce with those
who imitate our handiwork
but sweep away our homes.

"Dear friends," the wise old spider sighed,
"For webs of peace Arachne died.
Pray now with all your spider-hearts
and spider-minds to dedicate
your lives to help eradicate
the human fear of Spiderkind."

The congregation bowed their heads
and crossed their various arms and legs,
then crept away with faith renewed
in universal love.

III.

IN DIFFERENT LIGHTS

"The waves make a tour of the world,
I would like to go with them.
They have seen everything,
They never come back nor turn their head."
—Gerardo Diego

Warnings

What we know
can only harm us.
Filling our minds and souls,
it carves swiftly
into these hearts,
stealing our blood
for sustenance.

Dearest, we are in danger.
We cannot ask,
"Do we have the right?"
We must say instead
that poets
are the unlucky ones,
mixing breath and precipice,
gaze and need.

To survive, we must brave
the call of early mockingbirds,
immense in message and song,
pale mornings breaking lonely,
noonday's twist of brilliant light,
and always the wanting
wanting
wanting
destined to swallow us
whole.

Questions

for David Wagoner

Didn't I say that life was a climbing
from rosebush to mountain, from winter to spring?
Didn't I tell you that roses were summers,
that somewhere the moon stayed alive in the sky?
What I cannot recall is what I then told you
in trying to recapture the life we had known.
What I cannot remember is who did the asking
and who did the taking
and who did the falling
and what is my own.

Distancing

A fear of sudden waking, semi-conscious,
emerging from a blur of dream
to wear someone else's coat, murmuring a line
from an old conversation,
"The soul is vast, but finely tuned."

Half-sleep is needing to leave again,
to move unnoticed like a jeweler or thief
easing from gauzes of shadow to blackness
to flee disquieting light.

Down Jazz

Prisms resound, glow dissonant—
refracted word-dyes salvaged from malaise.
A bleeding swatch of rainbow,
cordless stains on muslin,
stacks of frightened tightropes,
my slippers thin and worn—
in tiny ribs of warning,
bits of ruined thread
disguise the floor.

Unfocused noise swirls resonant,
a mesh of blur and judgment—
bloodless prisms
edged alive with fear.
Unnerved by specks of soiled hope,
losing touch and balance,
I clutch a rippled strand
of severed air.

Hearing Your Name

Fall light bleached from red
to silver-white flame,
winter flickers cold
like sparks from a distance.
Autumn creates its own heat.

Fire rise sharp
in gestures of lightning,
microlight spears
burning through cloud.

Since spring
the clock has been faceless.
Neither of us
will ever
be the same.

Nightsong

I remember the quiet of the field that night
the quiet of our words
What we were saying
perhaps only the stars recall

Tonight the stars are out again
as quiet and alive as ever

Living a stranger's life
far from my father's country
I carry my past
on the palms of my hands

14th Street Bar

Feeling ripe and frightless
what I'm doing here tonight
is the part that doesn't matter
At the bar
men swigging hours of gin
a string of singing barstools
too little hope for mention

An aging sailor
shouts questions in French and Greek
a Cuban in black
bets his wallet on baseball
threatening to take down his pants
if he loses
promising he's never lost
before

In the morning
they will awaken somewhere
will remember only heat
and ice and glasses

Tonight they are a film
replaying a hundred other nights
Tonight
Lost in my need
I am a ceiling fan
noiseless
revolving

Words from the Woodshed

for Jimmy Giuffre

I.

Because you have chosen jazz over stillness,
    the dip and swirl of sound
        over silence,

I salute you for your courage
          admiring in your music
    a language
      too spacious
    for definition.

II.

Jazz   air   sailing
    climbing
    crashing
      blurred   light   reeling
              soaring
                spinning
    a musician
sway-
    ing: a
      private
          scattering of gifts—

Di Notte

This aria is from an opera libretto written for my composer brother, Vincent, who set it to music. It tells the story of a young Italian poet who falls in love with a German composer twice her age and defies her father's wishes by moving from Rome to Zurich to marry him. Their blissful marriage ends a few decades later when her husband dies and she is left alone to grieve.

The night we lost our hearts to each other,
It seems there wasn't a sound,
Not even of paper burning;
it seems that even the stars
were hiding behind the sky.

Symphonies, destinies, rivers and stars:
after so many nights of sleeping alone, when
always we dreamed of one another,
you called me your flower, your passionate Helen;
I called you my soldier, my sailor, my sea.
Each of us lived for the voice of the other,
a name whispered low from across a wide land.
Though our courage was careless, no one
could threaten us.
The night we lost our hearts to each other,
I gave up the names of my father and mother
and gave in—instead—to love.

For so many nights we lay without sleeping;
our breathing built houses of flutes and birds.

But tonight no breath is left but mine:
yours has ceased to sound.
Tonight the sound of our loving
that filled the room with softness
is an arc of polished sky above
a solitary row of trees.

Without you rain is only water.
Darkness is hard like a stone,
life a tedious climbing for light.
I am a stranger to hope.
Our primroses close in the noonday sun.
No swallows, no lutes. No sound but the silent
music of grief.

Each night I await your step on the porch,
your hands on the piano,
casting melodies from moonlight.
Instead I hear you enter my room, your lost voice
asking me something.

Though I do not reply,
you know well my heart:
we will be together, my love,
before winter
once again
begins.

For Eugenio Montale

"Only the isolated can speak
of the fatal isolation in each one of us."

Abandoned by September's changing dusk,
you left for a sun that rises alone,
more distant than shadows cast by stars
upon stars.

Still we are traveling forward, a race
denying the cry of your sister the storm
whose desolate warnings share courage with death
and the life signs you promised us.

In spring, when siroccos blow warm from the South,
from an African desert, from across a dark sea,
your words will return to us bearing the seeds
of the sturdy Magnolia, its unopened flowers
small walls of glory unwilling to fall.

Says the Taxi Driver

The sweet water
in Ecuador
is like a spell

When you drink
it goes straight
to your soul

If you drink enough
you're saved

IV.

GATHERING STRENGTH

"We wish on a star because a star itself is a wish."
—Rainer Maria Rilke

Evening Letter, 1996

I met a man today
>who jumps

out
>of airplanes

(that's right)
>he jumps out
>>on purpose

My guess is
he wants to fly,
>wants to soar, wants to
>>dip
>>into sweetness,
>into oceans of sky

as wide and vast and pure
>as the blue sea at midnight

or the desert at dawn
>or the heat
>of my desire

Midnight Drop Zone

When I didn't hear
from you
today,
I thought maybe
I only imagined you near me
last night.

Either that
or you have simply
left Earth again
      to skydive
      into
      someone else's
      world.

Are you some kind of Houdini,
I wonder,
or just a tall, smiling angel
sent down by God
to test my heart?

After the Encounter

Pull out the stops,
stretch the soul taut
for a moment:
after meeting her
it was harder and harder
to breathe.

As she nodded
and gestured
and rambled on
about herself,
my mind followed
the course
of her distress,
while my heart
(that wise medallion)
stayed at rest.

Now, hours later,
my feelings churn and swirl
before finally breaking free,
rising slowly skyward,
then spiraling down
in even, gentle circles
into the welcome warmth
of your embrace.

Evolving a Dream

To fixate on events and purposes,
to balance the Earth's axis on a nail,
to sing the scale of a silence
dream for dream,
to follow bone-sliver streaks of moon
that echo sheer at night:
in sparse light
in sparse light
in wish light
in sigh,
to turn quiet as a leaf turning bronze
in its time—
unnoticed, untainted
like a child in sleep.

Deep in the Mind of Noah

At nine years old
I swam in the ocean
and almost drowned

After that
I was terrified of water

At ten I was bitten
by two big black dogs
proof enough that animals
were not my friends

But when it came time
to save the world
from the Great Flood

I left my fear behind
and ran to get the dogs

Teacher

for Linda

When I was five
she taught me how to tie my shoes,
how not to miss a loop,
how to work the knot.

Now I lock the classroom door,
place books in young hands
gently

I warn the boys
(don't give too little)

I warn the girls
(don't give too much)

I lock/unlock doors
and teach them:
without the Muse,
the pen,
the sigh,
the willingness to pry open,
without the missed loop,
the tangled knot,
there is no growth.

To My Ten-Year-Old Neighbor

Six months ago you took it up:
the instrument your father played as a child,
coaxed by a mother not unlike your own
who believed in her heart that her darling son
would be a great musician someday,
or a doctor maybe, or a lawyer
who was so well-rounded
that every evening
after a long day in court,
he would return home
to play a few soulful notes
on a mean trombone.

Silent Hope

Drawing hope from a shallow, barren land,
naming want as the culprit of a cold dry winter,
I trace the theft back to Autumn
when nights followed noons too closely for light,
and days followed days through turnings that happened
from a spiraling distance
as we said they would happen.

On the last day of the last year
with nothing left to follow, nothing to begin,
still I will love you
beyond
all following.

Winter's Last Fling

Outside on the hickory
a nuthatch creeps
downward.
Sparrows lose interest
in my scatter of seed.

You too decide it is best
not to stay.
The next room pulls your voice
many miles away.

On Turning Forty

The world is not an oyster
nor my heart a hound
that chases an imaginary fox,
crashing through brush
and fallen pine boughs,
tearing up clumps of earth
as he races,
yelping wildly
into the night.

My will is not iron
nor my conscience as pure
as the water that surges
down the mountainside,
seeking the river
that leads to the sea.

My life is not simple
nor my feelings clear to me,
but like the hound and the water
I persevere—
now racing, now flowing,
now hoping my purpose
will make itself known.

Trying to Write

Along a deserted Arizona highway
I carry an unwatered plant,
squat down in a dry white glaze of light
to protect it with my shadow.

Somewhere
in some child's schoolbook,
is the answer
to all this heat—
to the parched brain,
the stillness,
the withered leaves of the poem plant
like strands of hemp
at my feet.

Italian Nights: Fearing the Yellow Rose

I.

Smokestacks spewing light
into darkening skies

flags in the rain

your disgusting beauty
ecstasy in tea leaves
an abundance of heart

II.

Olive women
yawning in the street

villas waiting
sleepless
beyond

III.

Soulbound

moonlight offering an inch
to crawl through

flying home   homeless
foreign eyes and all

IV.
What I keep forgetting:
blunders
birth scars
my uncle's patched face
my own hands
strange
eating from mended pockets
stuffed with air

V.
Sounds crossing streets
crossing darkness
these sparse thoughts
breathless shrieks
of still

Epiphany at Twilight

When hours become an ache inside my breast,
And life seems drained of every feast and song,
I think on those I knew and loved the best,
And those who left me here to suffer long.
When evening bows her head, she leaves but sighs
And miles of sky to follow in the dusk;
Shadows are her angels, moonlight her disguise
For every woman's face bereaved of trust.
Dear moon, no hour escapes us without pain,
Though your glow softens deep and joyless eyes,
And evening's nod accounts not loss but gain,
For in her dappled hours I realize
That love and dusk are but the names we've called
This small, brief life—a random poem scrawled.

V.

BLOOD TIES

"What can you do to promote world peace?
Go home and love your family."
—Mother Teresa

Letter to Mother

How is it possible you're dead, Mother,
when you look so alive
in the photo on my desk,
your father guiding you down the aisle
to meet the handsome young man
I knew as my dad.

They say you're gone
but I believe you're still here,
maybe somewhere far away.

Please send me a sign
and tell me where you are
so I can call you
and see how you're doing.

Shirley Wisdom

On her honeymoon at the beach,
my mother lost her gold wedding band
but never shed a tear.

"Love is not about rings," she said.

"It's holding each other tight
in a world you can't control,
or picking up a crying child
in the middle of the night.
Rings are for losing in the sea."

Silenzio, Per Favore, La Madre Dorme

for Piera and Vanna Canu

When the mother is sleeping and her gray hair darkens,
her small hands fold on her breast in a dream:
only in her sleep is she free of this city.
She is dreaming of Sardinia where her new house is waiting,
the cheese and the wine and the bustle of the market,
the mountains and the sky and the sound of the ocean.
Then she dreams of the room where her children were born,
the softness of the bed, the sweetness of the water,
the coolness of the bed sheets and the lull of the sea.
For a moment she remembers a child in her arms.

Later, done with dreaming of the life she had known then,
her small fingers shift in a hope for tomorrow.
She is longing to return to a life in Sardinia;
in the quiet of her heart's tranquil sleep lives this dream.

My Mother Loved Bunnies

Some scraggly gray rabbit would hop across the lawn.
"Look at the bunny!" she'd say,

And suddenly that little hobbling creature
was an aspiring movie star
waiting to audition for Peter Rabbit
or a bit part in Bambi.

Suddenly that furry form traversing the yard
was someone you wanted to know
or claim to know.
Suddenly you wanted that rabbit's autograph!

That bunny deserves your respect,
my mother would say,
for bringing moments of joy
and beauty into our lives.

That's how she felt
about all living creatures.
Yes, you too—
that's how she felt
about all of us.

Doors

"Close the front door—we don't live in a barn!"
my mother scolded my father
every morning of my childhood

"Okay," he'd say,
pulling the door closed
behind him

Other days he said nothing
and left the door ajar

I was too small to interfere
but liked the door left open
so he would come back

My Father's Deafness

My father is only as deaf
as the moment demands.

Like Rilke,
who kept his mind clear
by speaking French
when writing in German
and speaking German
when writing in French,
my father too
orchestrates his world:
it can be soundless if he wishes,
or humming with whispers,
or bursting with song.

The Power of Love

for brother Dan and his son Luca

Dad stayed alive an extra day
Waiting for the sound of the car,
The glow of headlights on the driveway.
He was waiting to hear your voice
To feel your hand in his,
To see Luca's face before him:
That was his last and fondest wish.

When you flew from Rome to New York,
And drove a rented car like a madman
Three long jet-lagged hours
To arrive at your childhood home,
You brought your father pure joy
For the first time in weeks
And a reason to stay alive
For a few more hours.

Though he could hardly speak,
Seeing you at the end
Was the memory he longed to carry
Into Heaven.

When you have moments of doubt, Dan,
As all of us do—
Close your eyes and let your father's deep love
See you through.

Rite of Passage

Please forgive me
for not knowing how
to help you die.

I brought you useless gifts
and kept going over the top
trying to be helpful,
but what did I know?

I was young
and brokenhearted,
terrified
of losing my beloved Dad.

Tenth Day of December, 1997

You can never get used to the fact
that your father is dying,
that you must say farewell to a man
who loved the people in his world
with a pure and generous heart.

You can never reconcile
the injustice
of your imminent loss,
or relieve the sadness
that rises into the night sky
to follow your father's soul
as it breaks free from Earth
to enter the glorious galaxy
of loving fathers
who smile down upon us,
ready to guide us
when we lose our way.

Grandfather Arcangelo

In those last days with us,
when your eyes no longer flickered with joy
even in the presence
of grandchildren,
you sat silent for hours
in your favorite lawn chair
beneath the sprawling red maple
in the backyard.

Though I was too young to remember you
strumming your hand-painted Italian guitar
or tapping your feet as your voice soared high,
then sank to the depths of your gypsy heart,

I do recall a nursery rhyme
you traced in circles on my waiting palm,
and how your hands fluttered in your lap
as you fell asleep,
and the sadness on my father's face
when you no longer remembered his name.

Memory never left you, Grandpa,
it just carried you far away,
back into the oily shop
where you made and mended shoes,
back into summer garden rows

where you lovingly toiled for food,
then back to the streets of Fondi,
the small medieval town
where you were born.

I still loved you, Grandpa,
when your gray eyes ceased to dance,
and with a small child's wisdom,
I knew you'd gone back home.
I told you stories anyway
and sang you little songs
and listened to your mumbled foreign words.

Oh Grandfather, Grandpa,
what difference did it make
that I couldn't understand
a word you said?

Sisters

for Carol Sue

Nothing momentous happened that day:
the wind did not whistle through our hair
as we sailed along—
sailed? Not exactly.

But as we moved along,
you—more secure than I on roller skates—
patiently guided me forward.

Behind us, your two small daughters
wheeled and giggled
and danced around the rink.

Behind us too,
          our childhood
did a tailspin,
          then a sweeping
figure-eight,
          amazed to see us
(after all these years)
still venturing forward,
holding hands.

When My Mother Spoke My Name

Turning back the hours, recalling all I know and knew,
I leave this night and wake alone
tucked in a small child's bed, my own.

The room is dark and spirits leap from window ledge to sill.
Above me on the ceiling, creatures trace my name until
I pull the covers over my head and try to disappear,
then close my eyes and hear the tread
of steps that tiptoe toward my bed.

My breathing stops as I cry out
"Don't hurt me!" to the figure there,
That's when my mother spoke my name
and cleared the creatures from the air.

The room glowed bright as morning
as she stood there smiling at my side.
"Don't worry dear, go back to sleep,"
she said and tucked me in and sighed.

The memory of that loving voice
that saved me in those early years
still keeps me safe on darkest nights
from doubt and lingering fears.

Adrift

When you lose a friend
you review your life,
vow to live better, promise yourself
you will never complain again.

When you lose your mother,
vows and promises
no longer matter.

Instead
you are cast out to sea alone,
saddened to the bone,
unable to cry out
or swim.

After Twenty Years

Nana has come back to whisper her secrets.
Nana has come back to warn against dreams—
back through the moonlight to walk in soft slippers,
back to reclaim the remains of her heart.

Now that I have shown you my past, she says,
once again it is safe to lie down in the forest—
to scatter my losses like the bones of a fawn,
to scatter my memories like pearls.

VI.

TERMINAL BENEFITS

"I have always imagined that Paradise will be a kind of library."
—Jorge Luis Borges

Journey

People keep calling this my cancer journey.
Even my oncologist used the term
as if I'd packed up my suitcases
and a few bottles of good wine
and hopped in the driver's seat of my old VW bus
to head to parts of the world
I might have missed.

With no bucket list of places to visit,
I drive aimlessly in one direction, then another,
stopping in little towns now and then,
looking anxiously for the faces of friends
who know what I'm going through.
Sometimes they call to send love and ask what I need.
I say I don't need anything
though I don't know where I am.

It's a lonely drive and I'd like to turn back
but the road behind
has disappeared,
so I continue on
directionless,
wishing I had a better relationship
with God.

Terminal Benefits

It's not so bad really

You eat whatever you want
Avoid people
you don't like
"Let's wait till next year,"
you say,
"when I'm feeling better."

It's kind of nice really
You look at the sunset
and beauty fills you up

How lovely, you think
I'll remember this forever

Hospital Waiting Room II

Everyone here is Lung
or Bone or Colon
or Unknown

Except one guy
Big shot, show-off
who keeps bragging
about Liver

I'm Breast Stage 4
I say nothing

It's cut-throat, this competition

Until Pancreas
returns from radiology,

I usually win

Concert

First the strings
tune up
louder and louder
till the cello's low groans
drown them out

Then come the sticks
tap tap tap, tap tap tap tap,
then the bass drum
thump thump thump thump
bam bam bam

Then more strings
Eeeeeeeeeeeeeeee
and deep-throated tubas
moaning the same fat notes
over and over

"You doing okay?"
says a muffled voice
from afar

I try to respond
but my voice can't compete
with bam bam bam
thump thump thump
tap tap tap, tap tap tap tap,
the MRI orchestra
playing my song.

From My First Avenue Window

Birds swoop and dive
between buildings
looking for openings
to climb to the sky

Filled with longing,
suspended between
good health
and death

I watch them
eagerly
find their way out

Waiting Game

On my abandoned desk
the flowers are dying,
scarcely yellow
after days untended.

No more watering,
no more pruning,
no more promises,
no more prayers.

No more plans, just wishes;
now that hope
is gone from my life,
from the depths of the sea
cry the fishes.

Stage 4 Quartet

I.

It's no use asking the stars what to do
They're busy burning holes in the sky
forcing hope
forever
out of reach

II.

It's hard to imagine non-being
no getting up every morning
no dressing for work
no hello to the neighbors
no worries or expectations
no wishes dashed
no wishes come true
no laughter
no music
not even one song

III.

Looking back at my life
memories disappear
like magic
I struggle to see them fade
but they simply vanish
No soft heat here
only burning

IV.

I wish I believed in heaven
instead of a physical death
when the mind
switches off
the body
loses sensation
and all the questions
I longed to answer
will float like burning embers
forgotten
leaving only
these words
behind

Next Spring

Of course I want you to miss me
when a white flash of swans
appears on the lake,
their tiny gray cygnets in tow,
and tricolor mallards primp and preen
on the lake wall below the wildflower garden
with its bright pink phlox, fragrant on summer days
and hardy coneflowers, black-eyed Susans,
and daisies too, their yellow faces ringed with white,
and a stubborn red rosebush that returns each year
to blossom in the crook of the white river birch
after the snowy winter.

In early fall, when the lake is as smooth as glass
and the morning sky is deciding what to do
with its rows of clouds, white streaks on blue,
making way for a day I won't see—
when the swans overhead
are teaching their little ones to fly
and you ask me to come and look,

Of course, my love,
of course I want you to miss me.

Acknowledgments

I'm grateful to my family for standing by me in all weathers, and to the esteemed poets who encouraged me to keep writing poems at various stages in my life—James Laughlin, Pawel Mayewski, Richard Eberhart, Donald Hall, Adrienne Rich, and J.D. (Sandy) McClatchy.

I'm also thankful for the love and moral support of my life partner for nearly thirty years, Scot Hadley Evans, and the many talented, generous friends who have inspired me along the way.

I appreciate the thoughtful assistance of Toni Robino, Doug Wagner, Autumn Wylder, Dan LeRoy, and Cynthia Poten for their help in putting this collection together. Finally, many thanks to Will Wolfslau and Lauren Magnussen at Amplify, who guided the book from idea to completion.

About the Author

Holly Peppe—author, poet, editor, teacher, and mentor—is a leading authority and literary executor for the Pulitzer Prize-winning poet Edna St. Vincent Millay. Her critical essays about the poet's life and work appear in the Penguin Classics, Harper's, and Yale University Press editions of her poems. Peppe also wrote an anti-bullying book for children, *Sophie and the Swans*, and co-authored two Scholastic books for young adults about Barrington Irving, the first Black pilot and youngest aviator to fly solo around the world, and *Mum's the Word*, a memoir about Eve Branson, British philanthropist, child welfare advocate, and mother of Richard Branson, the colorful British entrepreneur.

Peppe served as Director of the English Department at the American College of Rome, Italy in the 1980s before returning to Connecticut to teach film and literature programs for the National Endowment for the Humanities. She holds a Master of Arts in teaching from Brown University and a Ph.D. in English from the University of New Hampshire.

In addition to her literary work, Peppe represented individuals and groups committed to education, the arts, health issues, gender equality, and human rights in her thirty-year career as a global media, public relations, and crisis communications strategist. She spent eight years traveling to developing countries with ORBIS International, a nonprofit health organization, before founding her own PR firm in Manhattan, where her clients included the United Nations Office of Children and Armed Conflict. She also managed and promoted a diverse clientele including the acclaimed New York magician Steve Cohen. In earlier years, she taught music at an elementary school in rural Vermont and attended Woodstock, a treasured memory from her hippie days.